# The Dude De Ching

A Dudeist Holy Book
inspired by *The Tao Te Ching* of Lao Tzu
and *The Big Lebowski* of Joel and Ethan Coen

***By The Church of the Latter-Day Dude***
***(Dudeism)***

Illustrations by Colin Cotterill
Tao Te Ching Interpolation by Peter Merel


*Chiang Mai · Los Angeles*

# Contents

# Preface

After the Christian Bible, the *Tao Te Ching* is the most widely-translated book in the world. But that's only part of the story: There are no fewer than 100 translations *in English alone.*

This is because this Taoist holy book was written in a such a poetic Chinese idiom that no one can say for certain what it means. As a wiser fella than ourselves once said: "Sometimes you read the book, and sometimes the book, well, it reads you." The *Tao Te Ching* is that sort of book.

The Church of the Latter-Day Dude is heavily inspired by Taoism, and so it was that in the beginning of 2009 a few enterprising members of our forum started a *Tao Te Ching* interpretation of their own, translating it into the "parlance of our times." By this we mean they incorporated material from the film *The Big Lebowski*, one of Dudeism's more obvious influences.

After our compeers made it to the finals, the editorial board of The Dudespaper honed the verses a bit so that this here *Dude De Ching* would more closely match the message of the original Tao.

Here is the result: A book of levity and brevity which helps identify Dudeism as a modern incarnation of Taoism. Plus, to help illuminate the literal connection between the two traditions, the corresponding Taoist verse has been placed below each new Dudeist one. We hope you dig our style.

A big thanks goes out to those fellas from the forum who did the bulk of the series and set the ball in motion (Pastor Dirt and Digby's Kid especially, plus Laughing Dude, Digitalbuddha and Lone Dude). You dudes sure can roll. Also, thanks to Peter Merel for letting us use his lucid interpolation of the original Tao.

Gratitude as well goes out to mystery novelist/cartoonist, Colin Cotterill for providing us with the whimsical illustrations which help tie the book together. And last but not least, a special thanks to our very own Arch Dudeship Dwayne Eutsey for the far out *Innerduction* which begins on the following page.

Furthermore, this should be a living document, so if you see any room for improvement, please contact us and give us notes.

Dudeism abides,

REV. OLIVER BENJAMIN
*The Dudely Lama of*
*The Church of the Latter-Day Dude*

*Links:*

*Main site:* dudeism.com

*Online version of this work:* dudeism.com/tao

*Dudeism's official publication:* dudespaper.com

*Dudeism Forum:* dudeism.com/smf

*Illustrator:* colincotterill.com

*GNU for Peter Merel's Tao Te Ching:* chinapage.com/laolicen.html

# Inner-duction

In Dudeism's "Take It Easy Manifesto," we pose questions that fellas wiser than ourselves have contemplated across the sands of time:

> *"What makes a religion? Is it being prepared to do the right thing, whatever the cost? Isn't that what makes a religion? Or is it that along with a pair of testaments?"*

As for definite answers to these timeless queries, well, Dudes, we just don't know. There are just too many theological ins and outs and ecclesiastical strands to keep in our heads, man. Besides, we smoked a lot of Thai stick back in seminary, so, truth is, we don't remember a lot from our world religions class.

One thing we can say for certain, though: Most religions have a sacred book, a pile of holy writ that most adherents believe is the uncompromised first draft direct from God or what-have-you that really ties the cosmos together, wraps 'er all up. For instance, Jews have the Torah, in addition to 3,000 years of beautiful tradition from Moses to Sandy Koufax; Christians have Gospels that tell the miraculous story of how the Jesus rolled; and the fanatical cult of rich fuck reactionaries, well, they have *The Wall Street Journal.*

Scriptures, epistles, laws, prophecies, psalms, commandments, stock market analyses. So many learned men and women throughout the ages have disputed what they all mean, it can be quite stupefying. Even the religions that are some kind of Eastern thing—like Hinduism and Buddhism—have produced endless reams of Vedas and Sutras and rituals and chants and whatnot.

One exception to the whole divine-revelation-through-written-word thing, however, is Taoism. According to religious scholar Huston Smith, Taoism has only one basic text, the *Tao Te Ching* (or, in English, *The Way and Its Power*), a slim volume that, as Smith says, can be read in half an hour or a lifetime. Legend has it that a Chinaman by the name of Lao Tzu one day said "Fuck it" (loosely translated from the Chinese), hopped on a water buffalo (possibly with rust coloration), and started heading a-way out west to Tibet.

On his way out, someone stopped Lao Tzu and asked if he would write down the tenets of his ethos before leaving town. Being a lazy man, Lao Tzu lodged his water buffalo against an abutment long enough to write the *Tao Te Ching's* 81 short verses. When finished, he kicked his water buffalo into gear and, tossing his ringer to the man, rode off into the misty horizon of legend and myth.

Regardless of whether the legend is true, or whether Lao Tzu even really existed, the Chinaman is not the issue here, Dudes. The issue is that the *Tao Te Ching* is the perfect expression of Taoism's *wu wei* of life, or in the parlance of Huston Smith, a life of creative quietude in which "the conscious mind must relax, stop standing in its own light, let go" so that it can flow with the Tao (or Way) of the universe.

Dudeism has a lot in common with Taoism, of course, being its philosophical compeer. Taoists, for example, revere the fella I've innerduced by the name of Lao Tzu (literally "The Old Boy," not something most folks where I come from would self-apply); we have "The Dude." Lao Tzu rejected uptight Chinese imperial society and rode off to the mountains of Tibet, while The Dude rejected uptight American imperial society and became a roadie with Metallica. Lastly and most importantly, Dudeists share Taoism's *wu wei* ethos of just taking it easy, man, and rolling with the cosmic flow.

Although Dudeists have *The Big Lebowski* (a film you can watch in a couple hours or over a lifetime), Dudeism has lacked the equivalent of our very own *Tao Te Ching*...until now.

In this *Dude De Ching* that you're about to read, you have the perfect expression of Dudeism written by ordained Dudeist priests. While not riding water buffaloes to western climes like Lao Tzu (not for lack of trying, mind you), these priests have said, each in their own way, "Fuck it" to the stressed-out square community and have chosen instead to follow their inner Dude's calling to find some kind of metaphorical Tibet or Tao or whatever you call it in their lives.

You have your way of understanding a story and I have mine, but I think the best way to read these here verses we're about to unfold is to slow down, kick back, fire up a J or sip a Caucasian, and deliberately savor these stanzas as casually as possible. This ain't no spiritual In-N-Out Burger, Dudes. *The Dude De Ching* is just right for pondering as you soak in a tub surrounded by lit candles or when you lie on the rug that really ties your room together, digging some Dylan tunes or the clatter of your favorite bowling tournament.

After reading *The Dude De Ching*, you may say far out, man, I dig your style, or you may wonder what in God's holy name we're blathering about. Either way, it don't matter to the Dudeist. We can't be worried about that shit. Life is complicated and all too short and we're not interested in wasting it on dead doctrinal debates or stale ideological disputes. As one apocryphal Dudeist verse puts it:

> *The wind passeth over the flower of our days,*
> *Blowing ashes from a Folger's can back onto our faces,*
> *And it is gone.*
> *The whole concept abates.*
> *But life goes on, man.*

*The Dude abides. Nothing changes.*
*We take comfort in that.*

Aw, hell. I done innerduced this book enough.
Let's go bowling, Dudes.

Abidingly,

D. Eutsey

REV. DWAYNE EUTSEY
*The Arch Dudeship of*
*The Church of the Latter-Day Dude*

P.S. To our knowledge, no water buffalo were harmed in the making of *The Dude De Ching.*

Arch-Dudeship Dwayne's *Take it Easy Manifesto*
can be enjoyed at: dudeism.com/takeiteasymanifesto.html

# The Dude De Ching

## *The Verses*

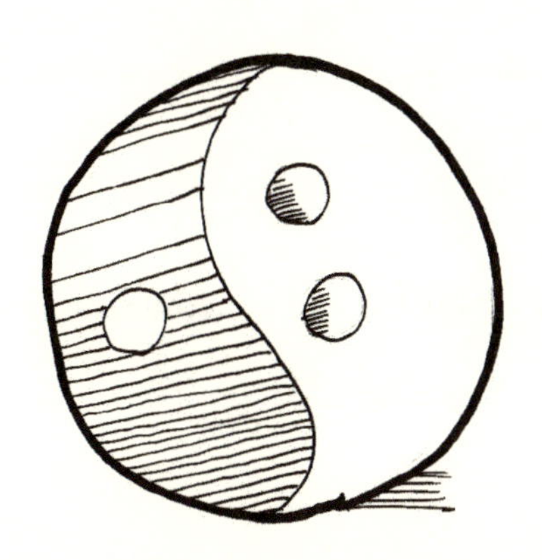

# 1. Dude!

Dudeness that can be known is not Dude.

The substance of the World is only a name for what Abides.

The tumbling of tumbleweeds is all that exists and may exist;

The rug is only a fabrication which ties the room together.

One experiences without being uptight, or enters a World of Pain,

And investigates complicated cases in order to understand the World.

The Dude digs the style of the Stranger, and the Stranger, the style of the Dude;

They are distinct only in front of the bar.

Sometimes you eat the bar and sometimes he eats you

Which is infinitely greater and more subtle than the fucking TOE!

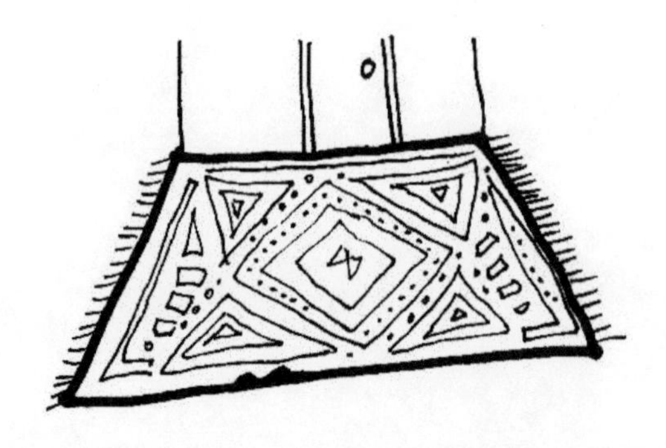

***Tao Te Ching:* 1. Tao**

The Tao that can be known is not Tao.
The substance of the World is only a name for Tao.
Tao is all that exists and may exist;
The World is only a map of what exists and may exist.
One experiences without Self to sense the World,
And experiences with Self to understand the World.
The two experiences are the same within Tao;
They are distinct only within the World.
Neither experience conveys Tao
Which is infinitely greater and more subtle than the World.

# 2. Style

When the Dude is recognized in the World
Undudeness is seen everywhere;
When Pacifism is hidden behind
Aggression will go unchecked.

Am I wrong?

In this way:
Amateurs and Achievers are abstracted from employment;
Complex and Simple are abstracted from getting down
to cases;
Toes and crossings are abstracted from lines;
Strikes and gutters are abstracted from lanes;
Reactionaries and Pacifists are abstracted from Our
Basic Freedoms;
Ups and downs are abstracted from the cycle.

The Stranger controls without authority,
And teaches without cuss words;
He lets all things take 'er easy,
Watches the semifinals, but does not interfere,
Drinks sarsaparilla without demanding,
And takes comfort where he can.

**Tao Te Ching: 2. Qualities**
When Beauty is recognised in the World
Ugliness has been learned;
When Good is recognised in the World
Evil has been learned.
In this way:
Alive and dead are abstracted from growth;
Difficult and easy are abstracted from progress;
Far and near are abstracted from position;

Strong and weak are abstracted from control;
Song and speech are abstracted from harmony;
After and before are abstracted from sequence.
The sage controls without authority,
And teaches without words;
He lets all things rise and fall,
Nurtures, but does not interfere,
Gives without demanding,
And is content.

# 3. Not Standing

Not achieving prevents having to overcome obstacles;
Not keeping the money prevents theft;
Not flaunting beauty prevents thousand-dollar blowjobs.
This is not 'Nam. This is bowling.

So the Stranger controls people by:
Digging their style,
Listening to their stories,
Telling them to take 'er easy,
And boosting their morale before the finals.

If people aren't privy to the new shit that has come to light,
Cowards among them will threaten castration;
If no action is taken,
There will only be pee-stains on the rug.

***Tao Te Ching:* 3. Control**
Not praising the worthy prevents cheating
Not esteeming the rare prevents theft
Not flaunting beauty prevents lust
So the sage controls people by:
Emptying their hearts,
Filling their bellies,
Weakening their ambitions,
And strengthening their bodies.
If people lack knowledge and desire
The crafty among them can not act;
If no action is taken
Then all live in peace.

# 4. Properties of the Dude

Let me tell you somethin' about The Dude.
He would never dream of taking your bullshit money;
You will not cut off his johnson, even if you throw a marmot into his bath;
His mind is limber, and he fits right in there;
What the fuck are you talking about?
I lost my train of thought here.

***Tao Te Ching:* 4. Properties of the Tao**
Tao is a depthless vessel;
Used by the Self, it is not filled by the World;
It cannot be cut, knotted, dimmed or stilled;
Its depths are hidden, ubiquitous and eternal;
I don't know where it came from;
It came before Nature.

# 5. Nihilists

Nihilists are not kind;
They believe in nothing.
The Stranger is not kind,
He drifts where the wind catches him.

Nihilists are like a bellows
Empty, yet full of hot air,
The more they threaten, the more cowardly they seem;
The Stranger also rambles and loses his train of thought
But tells a purty good story.

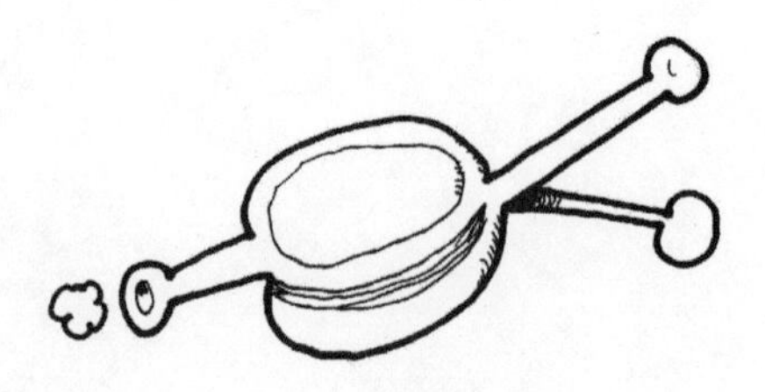

***Tao Te Ching:* 5. Nature**
Nature is not kind;
It treats all things impartially.
The Sage is not kind,
And treats all people impartially.
Nature is like a bellows
Empty, yet supplying all needs,
The more it moves, the more it yields;
The sage draws upon Tao in the same way
And can not be exhausted.

# 6. Bunny

Like a nympho stepmother, she has to feed the monkey.
She is commended as strongly vaginal, but makes no art—
Only beaver pictures, with ludicrous stories;
The Dude still jerks off manually;
Few bones or clams are found in his cash machine.

***Tao Te Ching:* 6. The Heart**
Like a riverbed, the heart is never filled
It is an ineffable female
Whose entrance is the source of the World;
Tao is ever present within it:
Draw upon it and it will never fail.

# 7. The Ball

Bowling is everlasting because it does not have a point.
In this way, the Dude:
Makes his point at the end and finds he made it at the beginning;
Rolls casually down the lane, and endures through strikes and gutters.
Because he does not put himself over the line, he does not enter a world of pain.

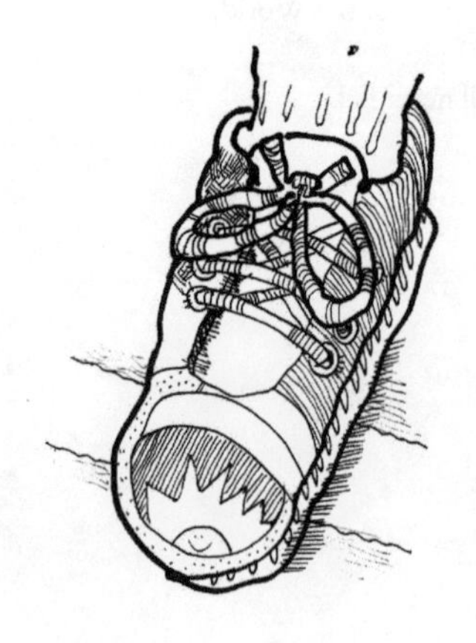

***Tao Te Ching:* 7. Self**

Nature is everlasting because it does not have a Self.
In this way the sage:
Serves his Self last and finds it served first;
Sees his body as accidental and finds it endures.
Because he does not serve his Self, he is content.

# 8. Digging

The man for his time and place
Takes it easy, and is calmer than you are,
He hangs out in bowling alleys and other places where
Careers slow down a little.

So the Dude:
In dwelling where it's already
the tenth,
In driving a car with rust coloration,
In helping his lady friend conceive,
In taking any rug in the house,
In patronizing the In-N-Out Burger
on Camrose,
In letting life go on, man,
In digging your style too—
He ends this thing cheap,
And harm is not visited tenfold upon
his head.

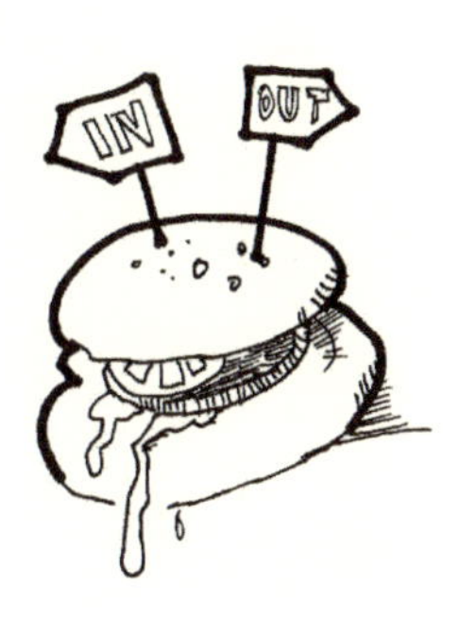


***Tao Te Ching:* 8. Intimacy**
The best of man is like water,
Which benefits all things, and does not contend with them,
Which flows in places that others disdain,
Where it holds fast to Tao.
So the sage:
In dwelling holds fast to the land,
In governing holds fast to order,
In talking holds fast to truth,
In dealing holds fast to men,
In acting holds fast to opportunity,
In crafting holds fast to competence,
In feeling holds fast to the heart;
He does not contend, and so is without blame.

# 9. Unchecked Aggression

When a plan gets too complex, everything can go wrong;
See what happens when you fuck a stranger in the ass:

Park in a handicapped spot, perhaps they'll tow it;
Roll your way into the semis, they're gonna fuck you up;
Take any rug in the house, you get a crack on the jaw;
Look for the one who will benefit, and they're gonna cut your dick off.

Say "Fuck it" – that's your answer for everything.
This is the way of the Dude.

***Tao Te Ching:* 9. Hubris**
Stretch a bow to its limit and it is soon broken;
Temper a blade to its sharpest and it is soon blunted;
Amass the greatest treasure and it is soon stolen;
Claim credit and honour and you will soon fall;
Retire once your purpose is acheived – this is the way of Nature.

# 10. Coitus

Embracing toes, you can blow that far,
Limber, sighing gently, you can roll a strike,
Loosening uptight thinking, you roll out naked.

Nurturing your special lady, you can take 'er easy,
Untying your robe, you become tied together,
Abiding with the World, you increase the chances of conception.

Mixing Kahlua and cream, but not soiling the rug,
Giving without demanding ransom,
Controlling without being a real reactionary,

This is a natural, zesty enterprise.
Oh.
Yes.

***Tao Te Ching:* 10. Love**
Embracing Tao, you become embraced.
Supple, breathing gently, you become reborn.
Clearing your vision, you become clear.
Nurturing your beloved, you become impartial.
Opening your heart, you become accepted.
Accepting the World, you embrace Tao.
Bearing and nurturing,
Creating but not owning,
Giving without demanding,
Controlling without authority,
This is love.

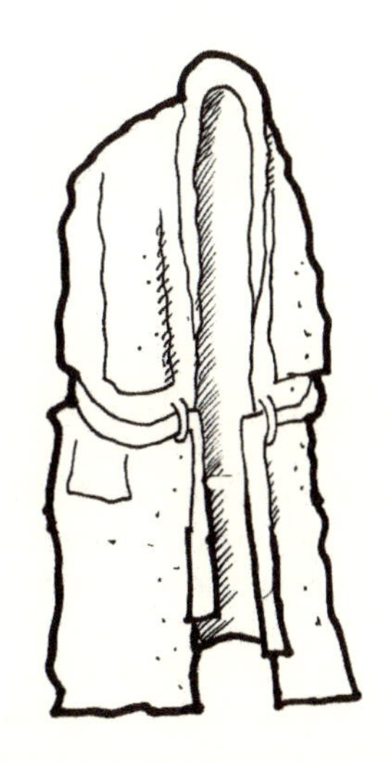

# 11. No Bottom

Twenty grand, man, meet at the hand-off;
They believe in nothing;
Dirty undies, the whites
Ensure the ringer will not look empty;
There never was any fucking money;
What in God's holy name are you blathering about?

Nothing is fucked here:
It is the receptacle which allows the remains to be transmitted,
And the holes which allow the bowling ball to be held;
What doesn't make sense makes it so durn innarestin';
The story is ludicrous. But it was a purty good story.
Dontcha think?

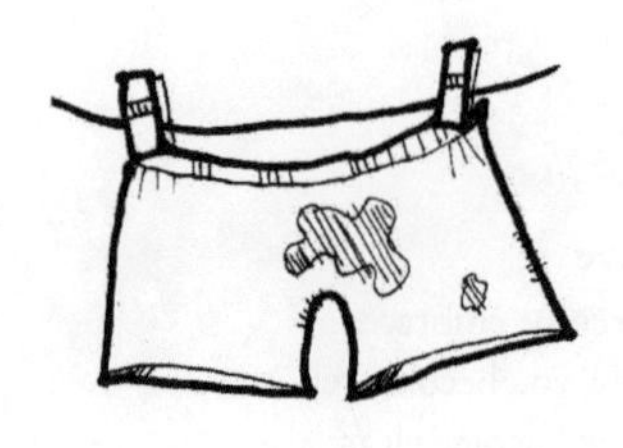

***Tao Te Ching:*** **11. Wealth and Worth**
Thirty spokes meet at a nave;
Because of the hole we may use the wheel.
Clay is moulded into a vessel;
Because of the hollow we may use the cup.
Walls are built around a hearth
Because of the doors we may use the house.
Thus wealth comes from what is,
But worth from what is not.

# 12. Beverages

Too much Kahlua blinds the vodka
Too much vodka deafens the milk
Too much milk dulls the beverage
Too much beverage maddens the mind
Too much madness makes the whole world go fucking crazy!

A good burger provides for the belly, not for the head;
In-N-Out, it pairs well with oat soda.

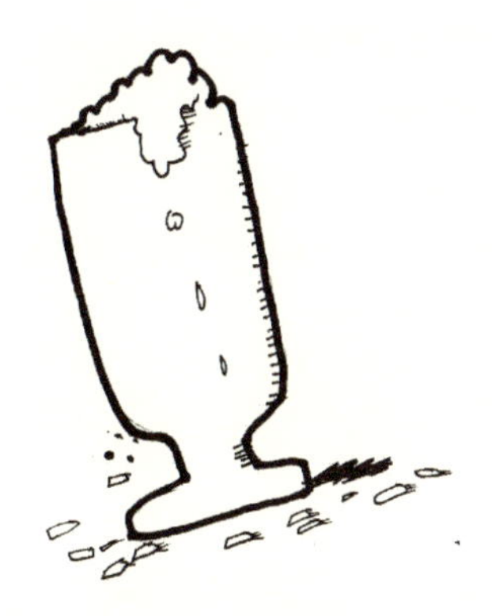

***Tao Te Ching:* 12. Distraction**
Too much color blinds the eye
Too much tone deafens the ear
Too much taste dulls the palate
Too much play maddens the mind
Too much desire tears the heart.
The sage provides for the belly, not for the senses;
He lets go of sensation and accepts substance.

# 13a. The Bar

The Stranger said:
"Sometimes you eat the bar and sometimes the bar, well, he eats you."
The Dude likes his style because he's got that whole cowboy thing going on.
That's the way the whole durn human comedy keeps perpetuatin' itself:
Westward the wagons. Tumbling tumbleweeds. Some kind of eastern thing.
I'm rambling again.

Therefore:
He who regards the whole world as the Bar is able to abide with the world;
He who asks Gary the bartender for another Caucasian is still racially pretty cool.

***Tao Te Ching:* 13. Anxiety**
The saints said: "Praise and blame cause anxiety;
The objects of hope and fear are within your Self."
"Praise and blame cause anxiety"
For you must hope and fear to receive or to lose them.
"The objects of hope and fear are within your Self"
For, without Self, neither fortune nor disaster can befall.
Therefore:
He who regards the World as the Self is able to control the World;
He who loves the World as the Self is able to nurture the World.

# 13b. The Dumps

The Dude said:

"You can't be worried about that shit. Life goes on";

"Would you just take it easy, man!? You're not wrong, you're just an asshole";

"My thinking about this case has become very uptight";

"I could be sitting here with just pee stains on my rug."

Of course:
You have to take the good with the bad;
Life does not stop and start at your convenience;
This affects all of us.
The Royal We.

***Tao Te Ching:* 13. Anxiety**
The saints said: "Praise and blame cause anxiety;
The objects of hope and fear are within your Self."
"Praise and blame cause anxiety"
For you must hope and fear to receive or to lose them.
"The objects of hope and fear are within your Self"
For, without Self, neither fortune nor disaster can befall.
Therefore:
He who regards the World as the Self is able to control the World;
He who loves the World as the Self is able to nurture the World.

# 14. Tying the Room Together

Looked at but cannot be seen – it is a worthy
fucking adversary;
Listened to but cannot be heard – it is a stonewalling
little brat;
Grasped at but cannot be touched – it floats off across the sky.

There is no bottom, nor the proper nomenclature,
All these strands make it a very complicated case.
In its rising, darkness warshes over,
In its falling, new shit comes to light:
A continuous blathering that cannot be told about.

Drawing a line in the sand,
It does not split hairs,
It throws out a ringer for a ringer,
There is no literal connection,
Down through the ages, across the ash-cans of time.
Not living in the past, but forgetting what day it is, and
abiding at the finals;
In this way, Dudeness perpetuates itself.

***Tao Te Ching:* 14. The Continuity of Tao**

The saints said: "Praise and blame cause anxiety;
The objects of hope and fear are within your Self."
"Praise and blame cause anxiety"
For you must hope and fear to receive or to lose them.
"The objects of hope and fear are within your Self"
For, without Self, neither fortune nor disaster can befall.
Therefore:
He who regards the World as the Self is able to control the World;
He who loves the World as the Self is able to nurture the World.
Looked at but cannot be seen – it is beyond form;
Listened to but cannot be heard – it is beyond sound;
Grasped at but cannot be touched – it is beyond reach;
These depthless things evade definition,
And blend into a single mystery.
In its rising there is no light,
In its falling there is no darkness,
A continuous thread beyond description,
Lining what can not exist,
Its form formless,
Its image nothing,
Its name mystery,
Meet it, it has no face,
Follow it, it has no back.
Understand the past, but attend the present;
In this way you know the continuity of Tao,
Which is its essence.

# 15. Great Dudes in History

The Dudefathers had understanding so profound
That we are like children who wander in the middle of
a movie.

Because we are out of their element,
We can only describe their style —

Good men and thorough, they never rolled out naked;
Ingenious, like a Swiss fucking watch;
Dark, like a black steer's tookus on a moonless prairie night;
Genuine, like Miller Genuine Draft;
Empty, like a modestly-priced receptacle;
Opaque, like a White Russian cocktail.

Those who can take 'er easy while lying face down in
the muck,
And remain perfectly calm while goons pee on their rug,
Aren't looking for a handout, nor do they need to feed
the monkey;
So everything works out pretty good for them.

### *Tao Te Ching:* 15. The Saints

The Saints had understanding
So profound they can not be understood.
Because they cannot be understood
I can only describe their appearance:
Cautious, like one crossing thin ice,
Hesitant, like one who fears danger,
Modest, like one who is a guest,
Smooth, like melting ice,
Genuine, like unshaped wood,
Empty, like a riverbed,
Opaque, like muddy water.
He who can lie still while the mud settles,
And remain still until the water flows
Does not seek fulfillment
And transcends Nature.

# 16. Tied Chi

Mix the holy beverage;
Embrace the rug that ties the room together.
Your arms and legs will rise and move;
Then return to rest,
All while sipping a Caucasian,
You'll be there, man,
Totally unspoiled.

Take 'er easy and abide:
It is the way of the Dude;
A string of ups and downs; strikes and gutters;
Understanding that the Stranger doesn't understand
Why d'ya have to use so many cuss words.

Who listens to sounds of the sea — whale songs,
bowling leagues;
Putting toes up while he bathes;
Feeling far-out, he smokes Thai stick in the tub;
Being magnanimous, though this is a private residence;
Going with the flow, he becomes one with the eternal
beverage;
Being one with the eternal beverage, he becomes privy to all
the new shit;
Though the drink will run dry, he can replenish it with ease.
—Is there a Ralphs around here?

### *Tao Te Ching:* 16: Transcending Nature

Empty the Self completely;
Embrace perfect peace.
The World will rise and move;
Watch it return to rest.
All the flourishing things
Will return to their source.
This return is peaceful;
It is the way of Nature,
An eternal decay and renewal.
Understanding this brings enlightenment,
Ignorance of this brings misery.
Who understands Nature's way becomes all-cherishing;
Being all-cherishing he becomes impartial;
Being impartial he becomes magnanimous;
Being magnanimous he becomes part of Nature;
Being part of Nature he becomes one with Tao;
Being one with Tao he becomes immortal:
Though his body will decay, Tao will not.

# 17. Achievers

The best Achievers are scarcely known by the Bums;
The next best are compensated and given beepers;
The next are real reactionaries;
The next, human paraquat:
They have no faith in the Bums,
So the Bums reveal them for the phonies they are.

When the best achievers achieve their purpose,
The bums leave them alone, mister.

***Tao Te Ching:*** **17: Rulers**
The best rulers are scarcely known by their subjects;
The next best are loved and praised;
The next are feared;
The next despised:
They have no faith in their subjects,
So their subjects become unfaithful to them.
When the best rulers acheive their purpose
Their subjects claim the acheivement as their own.

# 18. Losing the Train of Thought

When Dudeness is forgotten,
League bylaws and rules arise;
Then, political advocacy and pornography are joined,
And standards fall regrettably.
When you can't keep 'em down on the farm,
Then carjacking and Karl Hungus appear;
When the goddamn plane crashes into the mountain,
Fucking fascists will take over the beach communities.

***Tao Te Ching:* 18: Loss of Tao**
When Tao is forgotten
Duty and justice arise;
Then wisdom and sagacity are born
Along with hypocrisy.
When family relationships dissolve
Then respect and devotion arise;
When a nation falls to chaos
Then loyalty and patriotism are born.

# 19. Simple Plan

If we had 3000 years of beautiful tradition,
We would be living in the past;
If we were experts,
We could fix the cable;
If we had leads,
We would be working in shifts;
But we can't do that, Dude,
It fucks up our plan.

That's what we pay them for.
There's an unspoken message here:
Don't say peep;
Shut the fuck up, Donny!
Calmer than you are.

***Tao Te Ching:* 19: Simplicity**
If we could discard wisdom and sagacity
Then people would profit a hundredfold;
If we could discard duty and justice
Then loving relationships would form;
If we could discard artifice and profit
Then corruption and theft would disappear -
Yet such remedies treat only symptoms
And so they are inadequate.
People need personal remedies:
Reveal your naked Self,
Embrace your original nature,
Bind your self-interest,
Control your desire.

# 20. Mark it Zero

I know nossing and so nossing troubles me.
I see no difference between strikes and gutters.
I see no difference between ups and downs.
I do not fear bush-league psych-out stuff.

The people are merry as if at a Jackie Treehorn garden party,
Or rolling their way into the semis;
But I am easy and abiding,
Like a little Lebowski before it learns to dig,
Living alone, not much to tell.

The achievers are fuckin' loaded,
But I have nossing,
Also, my rug was stolen
And my car got dinged up a bit,
It was lodged against an abutment.

The achievers have never been more certain of anything in their life,
Where I am confused and rambling;
The people are strongly commended,
Whereas I throw out ringers for ringers,
Aimless as a wave drifting over the bosom of the Pacific ocean,
Attached to nossing.

The people are busy, as I know you are,
Whereas I am unemployed.
Let me explain something about the Dude:
He is sustained by the Tree of Life,
As the ex used to say.

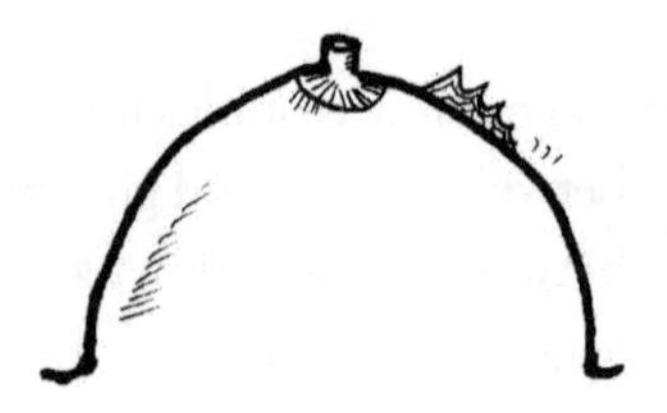

***Tao Te Ching:* 20: Oneness**

I know nothing and nothing troubles me.
I see no difference between yes and no.
I see no difference between good and evil.
I do not fear what the people fear in the night.
The people are merry as if at a magnificent party
Or playing in the park at springtime;
But I am tranquil and wandering,
Like a newborn before it learns to smile,
Lonely, with no true home.
The people have enough and to spare,
But I have nothing,
And my heart is foolish,
Muddled and cloudy.
The people are bright and certain,
Where I am dim and confused;
The people are clever and wise,
Where I am dull and ignorant,
Aimless as a wave drifting over the sea,
Attached to nothing.
The people are busy with purpose,
Where I am impractical and rough.
I am apart from all other people
Yet I am sustained by Nature, their mother.

# 21. The Three of You

The physical act of love is expressed through coitus.

The special lady talks a lot but does not listen;
Her art has been commended as being strongly vaginal;
Darkness warshes over, there is no bottom.

Vagina.

It expresses all that can be blathered about.

Yet without batting an eye a man will refer to his dick or his rod or his johnson.
That and a pair of testicles;
Don't be fatuous, Jeffrey,
Please slide your shorts down.

***Tao Te Ching:* 21: Expressions of Tao**
Love is expressed by following Tao.
Tao is evasive and intangible
But expresses all form and substance;
Tao is dark and subtle
But expresses all of Nature;
Nature is unchanging,
But expresses all sensation.
Since before knowledge
Tao has expressed these things.
How do I know?
By faith in my senses.

# 22. Can't Be Worried About That Shit

Abide and you achieve,
Spare and you strike,
Drink and you are drunk,
Take it up with the man, you got a man down,
A life of achievement, and didn't do very well at it,
Forget about the fucking toe!
Nothing about it indicates.

The Stranger accepts the World,
As the World accepts the Dude;
He narrates the film, so is clearly heard;
Does not self-apply a name, so remains unknown;
Has never been to London or France,
But can die with a smile on his face without feelin' like the good lord gypped him;
Because he does not eat the bar, the bar does not eat him,
He does not curse, so no one curses him.

The Stranger said, "Take it easy, Dude–I know that you will."
Yeah man. Well, you know, the Dude abides.
The Dude Abides.

### *Tao Te Ching:* 22. Acceptance and Contention

Accept and you become whole,
Bend and you straighten,
Empty and you fill,
Decay and you renew,
Want and you acquire,
Fulfill and you become confused.
The sage accepts the World
As the World accepts Tao;
He does not display himself, so is clearly seen,
Does not justify himself, so is famed,
Does not boast, so is credited,
Does not glory, so excels,
Does not contend, so no one contends against him.
The saints said, "Accept and you become whole",
Once whole, the World is as your home.

# 23. Blathering

The Stranger has done innerduced him enough:
The tumbleweeds do not last long,
Nor does the Dude.
If the Stranger's words do not last
Why should those of man, man?

To follow the Dude, become the Dude; the Dude will abide you.
To bowl, become the ball; bowling will abide you.
To lose the Dude, fuck off Da Fino; stop following him.
There's not a literal connection. Face it, there isn't any connection.
I guess we can close the file on that one.
Mind if I do a J?

***Tao Te Ching:* 23. Talk and Trust**
Nature says only a few words:
High wind does not last long,
Nor does heavy rain.
If Nature's words do not last
Why should those of man?
To follow Tao, become Tao; Tao will accept you.
To give love, become love; love will accept you.
To lose Tao, become lost; loss will accept you.
You must trust in order to be trusted.

# 24. Amateurs

If your toe goes over the line, that's a foul;
If you mark that frame an eight, you're entering a world of pain;
If you flash a piece out on the lanes, it will be stuck up your ass;
The fucking trigger will be pulled 'til it goes "click";
Fuck with the Jesus, and you are nobody;
If you don't calm down, you will be asked to leave;
If you don't have a fucking hostage, there is no ransom.

These behaviors are drags and bummers,
Disgusting things avoided by the Dude.

***Tao Te Ching:* 24. Tumors**

If you stand on tiptoe you can not stand steady;
If you stride too long you can not stride well;
If you display yourself you can not be clearly seen;
If you justify yourself you can not be respected;
If you promote yourself you can not be believed;
If you pride yourself you can not excel.
These behaviours are dregs and tumors,
Disgusting things avoided by love.

# 25. What-Have-You

Before the bowler rolls
There is mystery:
Silent, pinless,
Oil, boards,
Foul lines and balls,
The lanes of the World.
I do not know its name, so I call it Dude;
I do not give a shit about the fucking rules,
So I see what happens.

Seeing what happens, I can bowl forever
Bowling forever, the cycle is performed.

The Stranger follows the way of the World;
The World follows the way of What-have-you;
What-have-you follows the way of the Dude;
The Dude is the way.
Way.

The eternal Dude is infinite,
Therefore What-Have-You is infinite,
Therefore the World is infinite,
Therefore the Stranger is infinite.
There are four more detectives working on the case,
They got us working in shifts.

***Tao Te Ching:* 25. Four Infinities**
Before the World exists
There is mystery:
Silent, depthless,
Alone, unchanging,
Ubiquitous and ever moving,

The mother of the World.
I do not know its name, so I call it Tao;
I do not know its limit, so I call it infinite.
Being infinite, it flows away forever
Flowing away forever, it returns to the Self.
The Self follows the way of the World;
The World follows the way of Nature;
Nature follows the way of Tao;
Tao is the way.
Tao is infinite,
Therefore Nature is infinite,
Therefore the World is infinite,
Therefore the Self is infinite.
There are four infinities,
And the Self is one of them.

# 26. Calmer Than You Are

Gravity is not exactly a lightweight,
Calmness – our life is in its hands.

So Walter should not act compulsively or be a
real reactionary.
Acting compulsively, he waves a gun around,
Acting like a real reactionary, you're goddamn right he's living
in the fucking past.

The Stranger journeys all day without losing the trail;
Surrounded by stupefyin' things, he remains calm and orders a
sarsaparilla.
That's a good one.

***Tao Te Ching:* 26. Calm**
Gravity is the source of Lightness,
Calm, the master of Haste
So the leader of a great enterprise should not act lightly or hastily.
Acting lightly, he loses touch with the World,
Acting hastily, he loses control of the Self.
The sage journeys all day without losing control;
Surrounded by desirable things, he is calm and unattached.

# 27. Listening Occasionally

A good bowler leaves no pins standing;
A good tenant leaves the rent under the door;
A good husband leaves the toilet seat down;
A good friend leaves you the fuck alone;
A good caller leaves a message after the beep.
Takes a minute.

So the Dude digs your style
And says, "Fuck it."
He accepts everything
And says, "I'm sorry,
I wasn't listening."
He bathes with candles, whale songs, and Mr. Bubble.

Thus Walter must speak for Donny,
For Donny is like a child who wanders into the middle of a movie;
If Walter is not respected
Then no one will give a shit about the rules;
We enter a world of pain, and die face down in the muck.
Pacifism is not something to hide behind;
Many learned men have disputed this.

***Tao Te Ching:* 27. Attention**
A good traveller leaves no trail to be followed
A good speaker leaves no question to be asked
A good accountant leaves no working to be checked
A good container leaves no lock to be picked
A good fastener leaves no knot to be unravelled
So the sage nurtures all men
And abandons no one.
He accepts everything
And rejects nothing.

He attends to the smallest details.
So the strong must guide the weak,
For the weak are raw material to the strong.
If the guide is not respected
Or the material is not nurtured
Confusion will result, no matter how clever one is.
This is the essence of subtlety.

# 28. Being the Special Lady

Knowing the Dude, being the special lady
Being the lane through which rolls the Ball,
What is that, some kind of yoga?
It increases the chances of conception.

Knowing the new shit that has come to light,
Being the darkness that warshes over,
Being the balled,
She wants him to love her
But doesn't want to see him socially.

Knowing it's his fucking homework, but being perfectly calm,
Being the gutter for the Ball,
The physical act of love blows that far,
And one is as an unmixed drink.

When drinks are mixed they become beverages.
Used by the dude, they keep his mind limber;
Careful, man! There's a beverage here!
It's helping him to conceive.

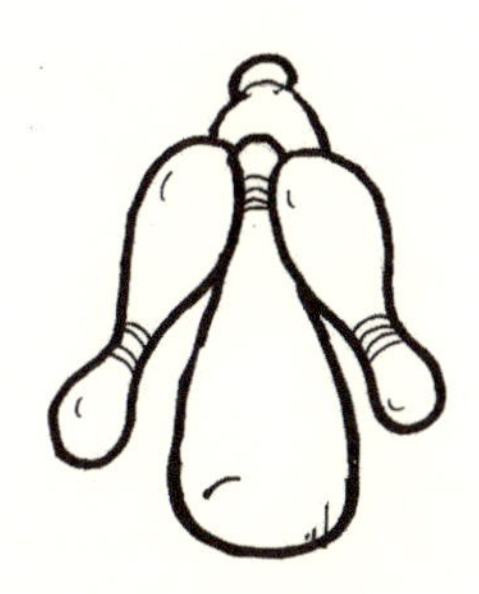

***Tao Te Ching:* 28. Being the Female**

Knowing the male, being the female,
Being the course through which flows the World,
One embraces unfailing Love
And is again as a newborn.
Knowing the light, being the dark,
Being the World,
One becomes unerring Love
And returns to Tao.
Knowing honour, being humble,
Being the valley of the World,
Love suffices,
And one is as unshaped wood.
When wood is shaped it becomes tools.
Used by the sage, tools become powerful;
So a good carpenter wastes little.

# 29. Fuggedabouddit

Those who wish to threaten the Dude
Because they want ze money
Cannot succeed.

The World is shaped by taking it easy;
It cannot be shaped by undudeness.
If one tries to steer it, the plane crashes into the mountain;
When one works in shifts, promising, uh, uh, leads will not be found.
Leads!

Therefore:
Sometimes we roll strikes,
And sometimes we roll gutters.
Sometimes you eat the bar,
And sometimes the bar eats you.
Sometimes people are reactionaries,
And sometimes they are pacifists.
Sometimes you take any rug in the house,
And sometimes you get a crack on the jaw.

The Stranger has never seen the Queen in her damned undies.
But he's seen something every bit as stupefyin':
What's a hee-ro?
This is our concern, Dude.

***Tao Te Ching:* 29. Blindness**
Those who wish to change the World
According with their desire
Cannot succeed.
The World is shaped by Tao;
It cannot be shaped by Self.
If one tries to shape it, one damages it;
If one tries to possess it, one loses it.
Therefore:
Sometimes things flourish,
And sometimes they do not.
Sometimes life is hard
And sometimes it is easy.
Sometimes people are strong
And sometimes they are weak.
Sometimes you get where you are going
And sometimes you fall by the way.
The sage is not extreme, extravagant, or complacent.

# 30. Aggression

Powerful men are well advised not to use aggression,
For aggression cannot remain unchecked;
Tumbleweeds tumble across any line drawn in the sand,
Doesn't anybody here give a shit about the rules?
Across this line you do not.

Walter is well advised
To achieve nothing more than the simple plan which is his charge,
No matter how many learned men have disputed this;
To defend our basic freedoms,
But to keep his voice down in a family restaurant;
To help determine who enters the next round-robin,
But not let his buddies die face down in the muck;
For even the worthiest fuckin' adversary will weaken with time;
He's cracking.

***Tao Te Ching:* 30. Violence**
Powerful men are well advised not to use violence,
For violence has a habit of returning;
Thorns and weeds grow wherever an army goes,
And lean years follow a great war.
A general is well advised
To acheive nothing more than his orders,
No matter how strong his army;
To carry out his orders
But not glory, boast or be proud;
To do what is dictated by necessity,
But not by bloodlust;
For even the fiercest force will weaken with time,
And then its violence will return, and kill it.

# 31. Paraquat

Goons are tools, violent, not golfers;
The Dude will not deal with morons.
His purpose is recreation;
Their purpose is micturation.

Nihilists are tools, threatening, ugh, techno-pop;
They are cowards, dipshits, crybabies,
For they are experts at unrepentantly betraying trust,
And taking ze money und calling it eefen.

Thus, those who lack an ethos
Will threaten castration,
Only to be chop-chopped themselves
From their toes, up to their ears.
You see what happens?

Say what you will—
A worthy fucking adversary should receive condolences;
Just as a dead friend should be celebrated with a eulogy.

### *Tao Te Ching:* 31. Tools of Violence

Soldiers are tools of violence, feared by all;
The sage will not employ them.
His purpose is creation;
Their purpose is destruction.
Weapons are tools of violence, not of the wise man;
He uses them when there is no choice
For he values peace and tact,
And does not delight in conquest.
For who delights in conquest
Delights in the slaughter of men;
And who delights in the slaughter of men
Cannot control them.
Slaughters should be mourned
And conquest celebrated with a funeral.

# 32. Leads

The Dude has no true definition.
Like Creedence, he runs through the jungle;
It's like Lenin said: Look for the one who will benefit.
Life does not stop and start—
Are we gonna split hairs here?

When the Dude is called Jeffrey,
Jeffrey is not the name of the Dude;
Too many strands in the head,
Allows the plan to get too complex.
Instead, let the Dude flow through Jeffrey into Maude
And the little Lebowski on the way
Who may or may not be the Walrus.

***Tao Te Ching:* 32. Shape**
Tao has no true definition.
Like unshaped wood, it has no use;
If a ruler understands this
His whole country flourishes and obeys
In harmony with his Self,
Just as sweet rain falls
Needing no instruction
To slake the thirst of all.
When Tao is shaped by use,
The shape gains a name in the World;
One should not keep too many names
Lest their shapes stop up the Self;
Instead let Tao flow through the Self into the World
As water courses down a riverbed into the sea.

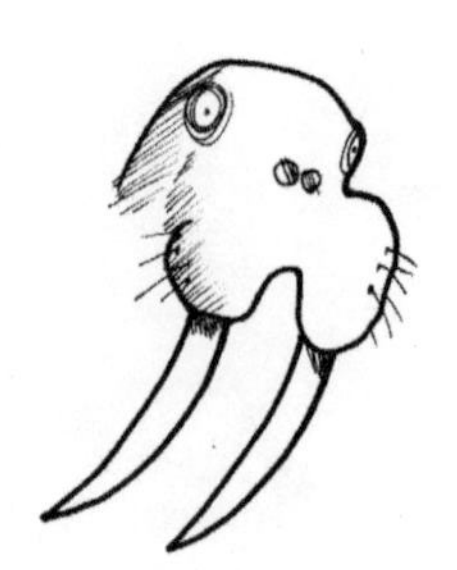

# 33. The Bosom of the Pacific

Who understands the Dude is learned;
Who understands the Stranger is enlightened.
Who bests competitors has strength;
Who conquers Nihilism abides.
Who doesn't worry about that shit has riches;
Who makes it to practice, makes it to the finals;
Who maintains his private residence will tie the room together;
Who maintains his dudeness abides, long after dying
Face down in the muck.

***Tao Te Ching:* 33. Virtue**
Who understands the World is learned;
Who understands the Self is enlightened.
Who conquers the World has strength;
Who conquers the Self has love.
Who is contented has riches;
Who is determined has purpose.
Who maintains his home will long endure
Who maintains his influence will live long after death.

# 34. Bottomless

The Dude is deeply casual during all the separate incidents:
Confronting Lebowski,
Attending the cycle,
Helping Maude conceive,
Wanting only for his rug in return.

He abides all things,
Does not try to scam anyone;
He is unemployed so he seems like a loser, a deadbeat,
Someone the square community doesn't give a shit about.

He is mixed up in all this;
In bed with everybody
He has no expiration date,
So he fits right in there.

Because it sees no literal connection,
Dudeness is bottomless, infinite.
That's marvelous, ingenious if we understand it correctly.
Very free-spirited.

***Tao Te Ching:* 34. Tao Favours No One**
Infinite Tao flows everywhere, creating and destroying,
Implementing all the World, attending to the tiniest details,
Claiming nothing in return.
It nurtures all things,
Though it does not control them;
It has no intention,
So it seems inconsequential.
It is the substance of all things;
Though it does not control them;
It has no exception,
So it seems all-important.
Because it favours no finite thing,
It is infinite.

# 35. Private Dick

The Dude lacks a job and business papers;
He can neither be hired nor fired,
Yet his services are highly sought after.

If you play the fuckin' Eagles and provide
lingonberry pancakes,
Morons may deal with you;
But if you comport yourself with Dudeness
The people will dig your style and understand your
unspoken message:
Oh, what a wonderful feeling!
La la la la la la la la la la la la la la la.

***Tao Te Ching:* 35. Peace**
Tao lacks art and flavour;
It can neither be seen nor heard,
Yet its application cannot be exhausted.
If you offer music and food
Strangers may stop with you;
But if you accord with Tao
The people of the World will keep you
In safety, health, community, and peace.

# 36. Under the Influence

To be under the influence, stop influencing the mind;
To make a crazy fuck happy, mark it zero;
To psych someone out, take a day of rest;
To win an argument, say "Fuck it" and leave.

This is the subtlety by which the weak overcome the strong,
For people should get paid in cash to avoid getting bumped into a higher tax bracket.
And little pricks should always stonewall fucking assholes.

***Tao Te Ching:*** **36. Influence**
To reduce someone's influence, first cause it to expand;
To reduce someone's force, first cause it to increase;
To overthrow someone, first cause them to be exalted;
To take something from someone, first give it to them.
This is the subtlety by which the weak overcome the strong,
For fish should not leave their depths;
And soldiers should not leave their camouflage.

# 37. Shut the Fuck Up, Donny!

The Dude does not act, yet leaves nothing undone.
When strangers understand this
All the Dudes of the World naturally flourish;
Flourishing, they are constrained by nossing.

Not greedy—
All the Dude ever wanted was his rug back.
And to take it easy, man.
Listen, you might learn something:
A peaceful easy feeling.
It's down there somewhere,
Let me take another look.

***Tao Te Ching:* 37. Quieting the Heart**
Tao does not act, yet leaves nothing undone.
If the Self understands this
All the things of the World naturally flourish;
Flourishing, they are constrained by Nature.
Nature does not possess desire;
Without desire, the heart becomes quiet,
And so the whole World may be made tranquil.

# 38. Religion

The abiding do not act.
Artists act to be commended as strongly vaginal;
Nihilists act to hide the fact that they're fucking amateurs;
The fig-eaters and Jewish Catholics act because it's all part of their sick Cynthia thing.

For when the Dude is undude, there is Jeffrey;
When Jeffrey is fatuous, there is Walter;
When Walter is a goddamn moron, there is Donny;
And when Donny is dead in the water, you need to brush him off your clothes.

Known pornographers are not easily fucked;
Belief in nossing is not easily annihilated;
Once the Jesus exposes himself to children
Their thinking becomes very uptight.

Ethos is the end of digging each others' style,
The beginning of not listening to the Dude's story;
Like a child who wanders into the middle of a movie
We are the Walrus;
And we out of our element.

The Dude's mind is kept limber, not uptight;
That's just, like, your opinion, man;
He sniffs the creamer before he buys it.
Carefully reviews all the labels and ponders them
Then chooses the most modestly priced option,
And pays with a post-dated check.

### *Tao Te Ching:* **38. Religion**

The loving do not act.
The kind act without self-interest;
The just act to serve self-interest;
The religious act to reproduce self-interest.
For when Tao is lost, there is love;
When love is lost, there is kindness;
When kindness is lost, there is justice;
And when justice is lost, there is religion.
Well established hierarchies are not easily uprooted;
Closely held beliefs are not easily released;
So religion enthralls generation after generation.
Religion is the end of love and honesty,
The beginning of confusion;
Faith is a colourful hope or fear,
The origin of folly.
The sage goes by knowledge, not by hope;
He dwells in the fruit, not the flower;
He accepts the former, and rejects the latter.

# 39. Wholes

In the early '90s things were not so half-and-half:
Business papers were more properly employed,
Our basic freedoms were more stable,
The peaceful were more respected,
That camel-fucker was a piece of cake,
Phones were not always ringing,
And the Dude abided.

But without credence, business papers are stolen;
Without basic freedoms, we enter a world of pain;
Without pacifism, our buddies die face down in the muck;
Without a hostage there is no ransom;
Without Saddam, the ringer is empty;
And without compeers, even the Dude wanders.

So the Dude depends upon the bowling team,
As the bowling team depends upon the Dude
They are the uncompromised first draftees,
A collective action of non-reactionaries.

Wholeness is made up of half-and-half:
Strong men also cry,
And deadbeats get down to cases.

Rather than ride the wave of the future
The Dude rides a '71 Ford,
The occasional acid flashback,
And the bosom of the Pacific Ocean.

***Tao Te Ching:* 39. Wholeness**
In mythical times all things were whole:
All the sky was clear,
All the earth was stable,

Allthe mountains were strong,
All the riverbeds were full,
All of nature was alive,
And all the rulers were supported.
But without clarity, the sky tears;
Without stability, the earth splits;
Without strength, the mountain collapses;
Without water, the riverbed cracks;
Without life, nature is barren;
And without support, the rulers fall.
So rulers depend upon their subjects,
The noble depend upon the humble;
And rulers call themselves orphaned, lonely or disabled,
To win their peoples' support.
Wholeness gains no support.
So there is weakness in power,
And power in weakness;
Rather than tinkle like jade,
One should clatter like stones.

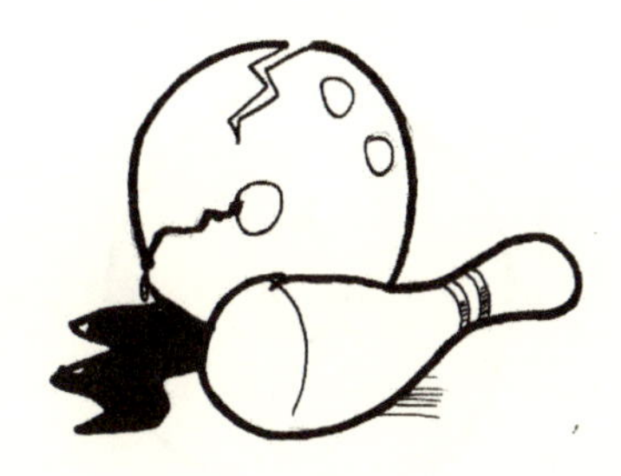

# 40. Application of Bowling

The motion of the Ball is a cycle;
The use of the Ball is to knock down pins which stand up again;
All bowling is made of Tao,
And Tao is made of nothing.
Well, that's your perception.

***Tao Te Ching:* 40. Application of Tao**
The motion of Tao is to return;
The use of Tao is to accept;
All things are made of Tao,
And Tao is made of nothing.

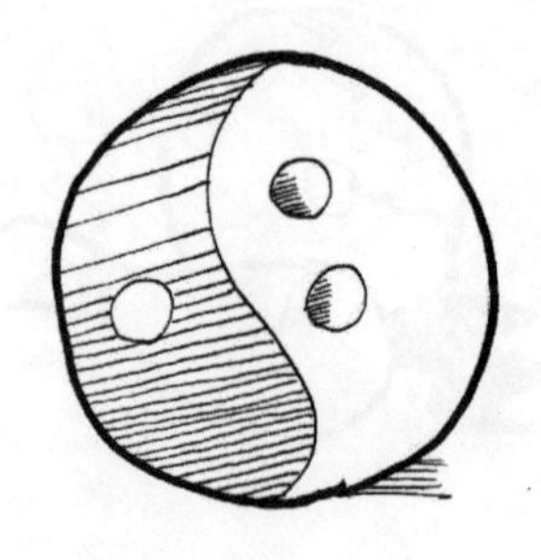

# 41. Dudeism

When the strong learn Dudeism, they practice it diligently;
When the average learn Dudeism, they practice it sometimes;
When the weak learn Dudeism, they take it easy;
Those who do not take it easy, do not learn Dudeism at all.

Therefore it is said:
Who follows Lebowski seems foolish;
Who progresses in Dudeism needs condolences;
Who follows the Dude seems to stumble and wander.

So the greatest stone wall seems like a pushover;
The simplest plan seems complex
The laziest deadbeat appears lively;
The biggest Lebowski appears meek;
The cockiest expert appears to be a fucking amateur;

So the rug, perfected, has no corner;
Art, perfected, has no johnson;
Coitus, perfected, has no interest in raising the child;
The female form, perfected, does not want to see you socially.

So the Dude cannot be correctly named or pinned down:
He transmits certain information, man,
And transcends his time and place.
Far out.

***Tao Te Ching:* 41. Taoism**

When the strong learn Tao, they practice it diligently;
When the average learn Tao, they practice it sometimes;
When the weak learn Tao, they laugh out loud;
Those who do not laugh do not learn at all.
Therefore it is said:
Who understands Tao seems foolish;
Who progresses in Tao seems to fail;
Who follows Tao seems to wander.
So the greatest force appears vulnerable;
The brightest truth appears coloured;
The richest character appears incomplete;
The strongest heart appears meek;
The most beautiful nature appears fickle;
So the square, perfected, has no corner;
Art, perfected, has no meaning;
Sex, perfected, has no climax;
Form, perfected, has no shape.
So Tao can not be sensed or known:
It transmits sensation and transcends knowledge.

# 42. Fitting Right in There

The Dude wears a robe;
The robe is worn at Ralphs;
Ralphs has the half-and-half;
Half-and-half makes a good Caucasian;
All things begin with thirst and end with a buzz,
But it is Ralphs that brings them all together.

As others teach, I teach,
"Buy what you need and nothing more"
Also, don't forget to sign up for a value club card.

***Tao Te Ching:*** **42. Harmony**

Tao bears love;
Love bears restraint;
Restraint bears acceptance;
Acceptance bears the World;
All things begin with love and end with restraint,
But it is acceptance that brings harmony.
As others teach, I teach,
"Those without harmony end with violence";
This is my teacher.

# 43. Solving the Case

The loser overcomes the achiever;
The bum penetrates the heiress;
The Stranger dies with a smile on his face;
Therefore, I value taking it easy.

Speaking without knowing
What the fuck you are talking about.
Action without work—
That's fucking interesting, man.

***Tao Te Ching:* 43. Overcoming the Impossible**
The soft overcomes the hard;
The formless penetrates the impenetrable;
Therefore I value taking no action.
Teaching without words,
Work without action,
Are understood by no one.

# 44. Abidement

Bullshit money or basic freedoms: which is dearer?
Contentment or competition: which is more valuable?
Compensation or employment: which is more painful?

Great coitus incurs great expense,
And great wealth incurs fucking phoniness,
But great abidement incurs no loss.

Therefore:
He who knows when to take it easy
Can't be worried about that shit,
And may long endure ups and downs, strikes and gutters.

***Tao Te Ching:* 44. Contentment**
Fame or Self: which is dearer?
Self or wealth: which is more valuable?
Profit or loss: which is more painful?
Great love incurs great expense,
And great wealth incurs great theft,
But great contentment incurs no loss.
Therefore:
He who knows when to stop
Does not continue into danger,
And may long endure.

# 45. Statements of Import

Perfectly calm seems imperfect,
But it's calmer than you are;
An ample allowance seems not enough
When it bumps you into a higher tax, uh—

Great stories make you lose your train of thought;
The music business attracts a bunch of assholes;
I'll tell you what they're blathering about:
It's all a show!
The ringer cannot look empty.

Though it increases the chance of conception,
Listen occasionally and you might learn something;
Don't say peep when I'm making a statement of import,
The uncompromised first draft.

***Tao Te Ching:* 45. Quiet**
Great perfection seems imperfect,
But does not decay;
Great abundance seems empty,
But does not fail.
Great truth seems contradictory;
Great cleverness seems stupid;
Great eloquence seems awkward.
Though action overcomes contentment,
Stillness overcomes desire;
So calm and quiet control the World.

# 46. Needing More

When the World does not abide the Dude,
Reactionaries throw their coffee at foreheads;
When the World abides the Dude,
Veterans enjoy their coffee in family restaurants.

There is no greater undudeness than to threaten castration;
There is no greater weakness than the weakness of vanity;
There is no greater ailment than a stress-related heart attack;
But one who finds it easy to take it easy
Takes 'er easy for all us sinners.
Shoosh.

***Tao Te Ching:* 46. Desire**
When the World is not in accord with Tao,
Horses bear soldiers through the fields;
When the World is in accord with Tao,
Horses bear horseshit through the fields.
There is no greater curse than desire;
There is no greater misery than discontent;
There is no greater ailment than greed;
But one who is content to be content
May always be content.

# 47. London and France

Without leaving your private residence
You know the whole World.
Without taking off your sunglasses
You know the color of the sky.

The more you dig,
The more there is to be dug.
The stranger wanders without a wagon,
Looks without seeing the Queen in her damned undies,
And rambles, without using so many cuss words.
In English, too.

***Tao Te Ching:* 47. Knowledge and Experience**
Without taking a step outdoors
You know the whole World.
Without taking a look out the window
You see the colour of the sky.
The more you experience,
The less you know.
The sage wanders without knowing,
Looks without seeing,
Accomplishes without acting.

# 48. Achievement

The follower of achievement acquires as much as he can every day;
The follower of the Dude just drops in to see what condition his condition is in.

By slowing down his career he reaches a state of inaction
Wherein he does nothing, leaves nothing undone,
Which bothers some men. Beaver.

To conquer the World, take it easy;
If you must do something,
Do a J,
And let the World conquer itself.

***Tao Te Ching:* 48. Knowledge**
The follower of knowledge acquires as much as he can every day;
The follower of Tao loses as much as he can every day.
By attrition he reaches a state of inaction
Wherein he does nothing, but leaves nothing undone.
To conquer the World, do nothing;
If you must do something,
The World remains beyond conquest.

# 49. The World of Pain of Others

The Dude does not distinguish between Lenin and Lennon;
He looks for the ones who will benefit;
This affects all of us.

He digs those who are a Lebowski;
He also digs those who are not a Lebowski;
That's terrific.
He does business with those who are wrong;
He also does business with those who are not wrong, but are just assholes;
He doesn't want to be a hard-on about this.

He is in harmony with the World;
So he abides the Worlds of others.
You know, it's just a game, man.
Mark it 8.

***Tao Te Ching:* 49. The Worlds of Others**
The sage does not distinguish between Self and World;
Therefore the needs of the people of the World are as his own.
He is good to those who are good;
He is also good to those who are not good;
For love is goodness.
He trusts those who are trustworthy;
He also trusts those who are not trustworthy;
For love is trust.
He is in harmony with the World;
So he nurtures the Worlds of others
As a mother does her children.

# 50. Life and Death

Death comes upon Donny
As the Dude comes upon Maude.

The limits of "The Man in Me" are this:
Thirty years of idealism;
Thirty years of Nihilism;
Thirty years in between, to abide;
So death and life reproduce themselves
Compulsively and without joy.

He who would just be sitting here with pee-stains on his rug
Will not meet Treehorns nor Nihilists nor Chiefs of Police,
Nor the other Jeffrey Lebowski, the millionaire.

So Treehorn would find no place to trash,
The Nihilists no johnson to cut off,
The Chief nothing to make plain,
And the Big Lebowski no deadbeat, no loser to pin it on.

As for the Dude, his days are as grass.

***Tao Te Ching*: 50. Life and Death**
Death enters life as man enters woman.
The limits of man:
Thirty years of growth;
Thirty years of decay;
Thirty years inbetween;
So death and life reproduce themselves.
He who would prolong his life
Will not meet tigers or rhinoceri in the wilds,
Nor soldiers in battle
So the rhinoceros finds no place in him for its horn,
The tiger no place for its claw,
The soldier no place for a weapon;
So death finds no place to enter his life.

# 51. Abiding

Strong vaginas command us,
Private dicks snoop around behind us,
Cleft assholes laugh at us,
New shit comes to light, and occurs to us.

We abide and honor the Dude;
For abiding and honoring the Dude
Are performed by not being a fucking asshole.

The Dude abides—
Abiding sympathizes,
Slips the rent under the door,
Drives us to Pasadena,
Does not make us saps
And forgets about the fucking TOE.

Bowling without controlling;
Dying without feelin' like the good Lord gypped you;
Not promising without the necessary means for a necessary means;
Getting called a jerkoff but not listening;
This is abiding.

***Tao Te Ching:* 51. Love**

Tao bears us,
Love nurtures us,
Nature shapes us,
Circumstance completes us.
We worship Tao and honour love;
For worship of Tao and honour of love
Are performed by being alive.
Tao bears us,
Love nurtures, develops, cares for,
Shelters, comforts, and makes a home for us.
Making without controlling,
Giving without demanding,
Guiding without interfering,
Helping without profiting,
This is love.

# 52. Prior Restraint

The origins of the Dude are in the Port Huron Statement;
Know its time and place, and you understand the Dude;
Read the uncompromised first draft;
You can imagine where it went from there;
The bums lost.

Keep your voice down in a family restaurant
And you maintain your dudeness;
Make everything a first amendment issue
And everything's a fucking travesty with you, man.

Father's weakness is vanity
Do you have to use so many cuss words
When you're trying to do business here, man?
Fuck it. Have it your way, Dude.
The Supreme Court has roundly rejected prior restraint.

***Tao Te Ching:* 52. Restraint**
The origins of the World are its mother;
Know the mother, and you understand the child;
Know the child, and you embrace the mother,
Who shall not perish when you die.
Reserve your judgments and words
And you maintain your influence;
Draw conclusions and speak your mind
And your cause is lost.
As seeing detail is clarity,
So maintaining tact is strength;
Keep your eyes and mind open
So that you may not regret your actions;
This is restraint.

# 53. Feeding the Monkey

With but the modest task which is your charge
One may follow the Dude like a Brother Shamus,
Fearing only that you'll fuck it up;
Yet while following instructions is easy,
believing in nossing is also easy.
That's two things we learned in 'Nam.

When Pasadena is well-kept
The Valley is left to tumbleweeds;
When the bowling alleys are empty.
Darkness warshes over.

Wearing purple jumpsuits,
Recording German techno-pop,
Fucking a stranger in the ass,
Keeping amphibious rodents within the city limits—
These are the ways of the monkey-feeders
And deviations from the Dude.

***Tao Te Ching:* 53. Distractions**
With but a small understanding
One may follow Tao like a main road,
Fearing only to leave it;
Following a main road is easy,
But being sidetracked is also easy.
When palaces are kept up
Fields are left to weeds
And granaries empty.
Wearing fine clothes,
Bearing sharp swords,
Glutting with food and drink,
Hoarding wealth and possessions -
These are the ways of theft
And deviation from Tao.

## 54. Love in the True Sense of the Word

The Dude does not think of the Dude
For this reason he abides;
He does nothing,
Yet leaves nothing undone.

Nihilists want that fucking money,
For this reason they are a bunch of cry-babies;
They always act,
Yet get nossing done.

Nurture love in the true sense of the word,
And you won't try to scam anyone here;
Nurture love in the residence,
And it will tie the room together;
Nurture love in the bowling team,
And it will make it to the finals;
Nurture love in your time and place,
And you'll fit right in there;
Nurture love in the World,
And that about wraps her all up.

Therefore:
Know a person by their love;
Know a residence by its love;
Know a bowling team by its love;
Know a time and place by its love;
Know the World by its love.
How can I enter a world of no-pain?
By loving the World,
Even when it's full of goddamn morons.

***Tao Te Ching:* 54. Go by Love**

Love does not think of love
For this reason is it strong;
It does not act,
Yet leaves nothing undone.
Desire is intent upon love
For this reason is it weak;
It always acts,
Yet gets nothing done.
Nurture love in the Self, and love will be genuine;
Nurture love in the family, and love will be abundant;
Nurture love in the community, and love will multiply;
Nurture love in the culture, and love will flourish;
Nurture love in the World, and love will be ubiquitous.
Therefore:
Judge a person by their love;
Judge a family by its love;
Judge a community by its love;
Judge a culture by its love;
Judge the World by its love.
How can I know the love of the World?
By judging my Self.

# 55. A Natural, Zesty Enterprise

Who is filled with love is like the Dude.
Marmots will not scare him;
Pomeranians will not take his turn at bowling;
Nihilists will not cut off his johnson.

His belly is soft, yet his toes are supple,
So he rolls a strike;
He has no wife, you see no ring on his finger,
The toilet seat is up;
He sings the theme to "Branded" in a Malibu patrol car,
And his harmony is perfect.

To approach Nature is to know the Dude;
To be enterprising and zesty is natural;
But to surpass the Dude is to enter a world of pain
For too many Js will burn the lungs
And too much half-and-half will age the heart;
The toe that slips over the line may get cut off,
Making it difficult to enjoy wearing sandals.

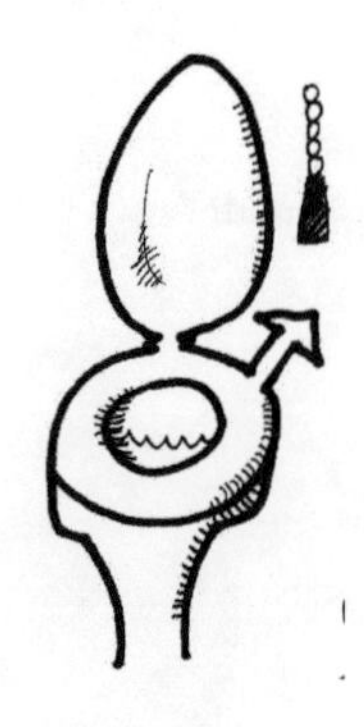

***Tao Te Ching:* 55. Love and Nature**

Who is filled with love is like a newborn.
Wasps will not sting him;
Tigers will not eat him;
Hawks will not tear out his eyes.
His bones are soft, yet his sinews are supple,
So his grip is strong;
He has no wife, yet his manhood is healthy,
So his vigour is unspoiled;
He sings all day yet his voice remains sweet
So his harmony is perfect.
To approach Nature is to know harmony;
To acheive Nature is to be enlightened;
But to surpass Nature invites calamity
For emotion will burst the lungs
And exhaustion will age the heart;
The light that burns twice as bright
Burns half as long.

# 56. That's Cool. That's Cool

He who knows does not blather;
He who blathers should not say peep when I'm doing business.
It's just, like, your opinion, man,
Keep your voice down
And stay out of complicated cases;
There's an unspoken message here—
It's "shut the fuck up!"

In shutting the fuck up,
Friendship and aggression,
Profit and loss,
Strikes and gutters,
Will not affect you.
Why don't you fucking listen occasionally?
You might learn something.

***Tao Te Ching:* 56. Impartiality**
He who knows does not speak;
He who speaks does not know.
Reserve your judgments and words;
Dull your wit and simplify your purpose;
Be humble as earth and a part of Nature.
In this way
Friendship and enmity,
Profit and loss,
Honour and disgrace,
Will not affect you.
The impartial Self is of most benefit to the World.

# 57. The President

A bowling league is best governed by Donny;
A war is best waged by fig eaters trying to find reverse on a Soviet Tank;
The World is best controlled by taking it easy;
Why?

Because:
The more competition and achievement there is,
The more the bums lose;
The more guns there are to be waved around,
The more league bylaws are contravened;
The more strongly beaver pictures are commended,
The more we cannot love in the true sense of the word;
The more nice, quiet little beach communities are built,
The more lines will be drawn in the sand.

Therefore the Stranger says:
I take it easy, and the whole durned human comedy is perpetuated;
I hitch my wagon westward and people become surfers;
I lose my train of thought and the story unfolds anyway;
I innerduce the Dude, and the World digs my style.

***Tao Te Ching:* 57. Government**

A nation is best governed by innocence;
A war is best waged by treachery;
The World is best controlled by inaction;
Why?
Because:
The more property and taxes there are,
The more poverty prevails;
The more guns and knives there are,
The more chaos prevails;
The more arts and sciences there are,
The more deceit prevails;
The more rules and regulations there are,
The more theft prevails.
Therefore the sage says:
I take no action, and the people become civilized;
I wage no war, and the people become just;
I transact no business, and the people become wealthy;
I have no desire, and the people become innocent.

# 58. Not a Problem

When the Dude is lazy and smokes blunts
The people are friendly and cool;
When Walter is adversarial and not fucking around
The people stonewall and deceive.

Bummers may yield happiness;
Happiness may conceal tears.
Who can say what makes a man?
Let me tell you something, *pendejo* –
Drafts are always compromised;
Helluva Caucasians are ever offered;
Men have always been like this, down through the ages.

So the Stranger is firm but not cussing,
Polite but not a pervert,
Named but not known,
A smarter feller than ourselves,
Though that's not a handle he would self-apply.

**_Tao Te Ching:_ 58. Be Forgiving**

When government is lazy and blunt
The people are kind and honest;
When government is efficient and severe
The people are discontented and deceitful.
Misery may yield happiness;
Happiness may conceal misery.
Who can say which will be for the best?
Nothing is straightforward.
Honesty is ever corrupted;
Kindness is ever seduced;
Men have been like this for a long time.
So the sage is firm but not cutting,
Pointed but not piercing,
Straight but not inflexible,
Brilliant but not blinding.

# 59. Put the Piece Away

Solve a complicated case
As you would smoke a J.

When directing men to a purpose
The sage tells them not to fuck around;
Restraint allows time
For story, production value, feelings,
To bowl and to bathe,
To simplify the plan,
To help her conceive;
With Kahlua and kindness, aggression will not stand;
When aggression will not stand, our fucking troubles are over.

Who can abide is able to direct men
And they all remain under the influence.
Tied together with limber minds,
His style remains, even after the last strike is rolled.

***Tao Te Ching:* 59. Restraint**
Manage a great nation
As you would cook a delicate fish.
When directing men to a purpose
The sage is restrained;
Restraint allows time to prepare and strengthen,
To build loving relationships;
With sufficient strength and love all resistance is overcome;
When all resistance is overcome one's purpose is acheived.
Who can acheive his purpose is able to direct men
And his influence upon them long endures.
Deeply rooted and firmly established,
His vision lives on even after death.

# 60. Words

Because the Stranger allows, his Words do not bother some men;
It is not that they lack true sense
But that they do not have a literal connection.
Because there is no literal connection
You have it your way, Dude.
Because you have it your way,
Dudes take comfort in their conversations with him.

***Tao Te Ching:* 60. Emotions**
Because the sage follows Tao his emotions do no harm;
It is not that they lose their power
But that they do not hurt others;
Because they do not hurt others
He does not hurt others:
Because his emotions do no harm,
All his relations with people are loving.

# 61. Love Me

A society ties the people together through seduction;
Maude seduces the Dude by slipping off her robe
Even though it was not hers to slip.

When the Dude submits to Maude
He does so to compulsively fornicate;
When Maude submits to the Dude
She does so because she wants a child;
The Dude will submit for fun and games
Maude will submit to increase the chances of conception.

Therefore:
It is in everyone's interest to pool their resources,
Trade information, compeers, you know?
To achieve the modest tasks which are our charge,
We must resign to be tender.

***Tao Te Ching:* 61. International Relations**

A nation acts as a hierarchy, a community, and a woman.
A woman seduces a man by being cool,
Being cool is a means of submission.
If a large country submits to a small country
It will seduce the small country;
If a small country submits to a large country
It will seduce the large country;
The large will submit in order to control
And the small will submit in order to prosper.
Therefore:
It is in the interests of a large country to give shelter,
And in the interests of a small country to give service;
If both would acheive their purposes,
Both must submit.

# 62. Sinners

The Dude is the source of all things,
The comfort of the Stranger,
And the easy-taker for the sinner.

A true sense of the words wins honor
And a worthy fuckin' adversary wins respect,
But if a man is fragile, very fragile, do not abandon him;
And if a man accomplishes more than most men, do not dream of taking his bullshit money;
Just take it easy, and promise to be there, man—
To give him notes;
To sympathize here;
To help put him back in the chair.

Why is the Dude the comfort of the Stranger?
Because his style is likeable.
Why is the Dude the easy-taker for the sinner?
Because he loves you even if you're a goddamn moron.
It is the most modest price.

***Tao Te Ching:* 62. Sin**
Tao is the source of all things,
The treasure of the saint,
And the refuge of the sinner.
Fine words win honour
And fine actions win respect,
But if a man sins, do not abandon him;
And if a man gains power, do not bribe him;
Just be calm and show accordance with Tao.
Why is Tao the treasure of the saint?
Because it absolves all sin.
Why is Tao the refuge of the sinner?
Because it is easily found when sought.
It is the most valuable gift.

# 63. Obstacles Overcome

Practice not practicing;
Attend to modest tasks;
Sample discounted half-and-half,
Cherish the smallest roach,
Don't roll on Shabbos,
Mark it Zero.

Deal with the plan while it is still simple:
Too many strands in old Duder's head make his thinking uptight.
When a plan gets too complex, everything can go wrong.
Vladimir Ilyich Ulyanov!

So the Dude, in not worrying about that shit,
Figures out where the money isn't.
He who forgets about the fucking toe enjoys his coffee;
He who takes things lightly, abides all things.

The Dude does not confront difficulty, and so has none.

**_Tao Te Ching:_ 63. Confront Difficulty**

Practise no-action;
Attend to do-nothing;
Taste the flavorless,
Examine the small,
Multiply the few,
Return love for hate.
Deal with difficulty while it is yet easy;
Deal with the great while it is yet small;
The difficult develops naturally from the easy
And the great from the small;
So the sage, by dealing with the small
Acheives the great.
He who finds it easy to promise finds it hard to deliver;
He who takes things lightly makes things hard;
The sage confronts difficulty, and so has none.

# 64a. Care at the Approach

Hold the bowling ball still, so it is easy to grasp;
The obstacles do not move, so are easy to aim at;
The lane is slick, so easy to roll upon;
The pins are not braced, so should be a push over.

Yet,
A roll that hooks too hard can cause a split;
A ball that slides too far can flow into the gutter;
A journey of sixty feet begins at the spot under one's toe.

Therefore roll your way into the semis before making it to the finals;
Pretend you are bowling while relaxing on your rug;
Knock down the pins before you even release the ball.

***Tao Te Ching:* 64a. Care at the Beginning**
What lies still is easy to grasp;
What is far off is easy to anticipate;
What is cold is easy to shatter;
What is small is easy to disperse.
Yet,
A tree broader than a man can embrace is born of a tiny shoot;
A dam taller than a river can overflow is based on a clod of earth;
A journey of a thousand miles begins at the spot under one's feet.
Therefore deal with things before they happen;
Create order before there is confusion.

# 64b. Care at the Follow-through

He who strives, splits;
He who grasps, gutters.
People often split on the verge of a strike;
Take care at the follow-through as you did at the approach,
So that you may eternally throw rocks.

The Dude desires no desire,
Only wants his rug back,
Remembers nothing from college,
But teaches people how to take it easy
He does his best to make it to the finals
Without being a crazy fuck.

***Tao Te Ching:* 64b. Care at the End**
He who acts, spoils;
He who grasps, loses.
People often fail on the verge of success;
Take care at the end as at the beginning,
So that you may avoid failure.
The sage desires no desire,
Values no valuable,
Knows no knowledge,
But gives people what they can not find
And helps all things accord with Nature
Without interfering.

# 65. History Class

The Stranger did not want to make the Dude wise,
But only to take comfort in his style;
After all, sometimes you eat the bar, and sometimes the bar eats you.

To insist that someone's beautiful tradition is all just a part of their sick Cynthia thing
Only keeps them living in the past.
Becoming privy to the new shit
Helps perpetuate the whole durn human comedy.

Understanding these two scenes is understanding history;
Understanding history keeps all the strands in your head
In order that we may see through fucking phonies
And help them up.

**_Tao Te Ching:_ 65. History**

The saints did not want to make people wise,
But to make them ignorant;
For it is difficult to lead people who know too much.
To lead a nation by imparting knowledge to its people
Destroys the nation.
To lead a nation by decreasing the knowledge of its people
Strengthens the nation.
Understanding these two paths is understanding history;
Understanding history gives clarity of vision
By which one may see through deceit.

# 66. Following Around

How did the river carve out Simi Valley?
By flowing beneath it.
Thereby the river is master of Simi Valley.

In order to master people
One must speak as a loser or a deadbeat;
So when the Dude is elevated to power
People say, "Far out."

In order to lead people
One must follow them.
So that everybody will dig the Dude's work,
He gets in bed with everybody,
Increasing their chances of conception.

Thus the Dude abides without fail,
He does not seem superior, so no one will stonewall him.
He listens and learns,
Eyeball to eyeball,
And fits right in there.

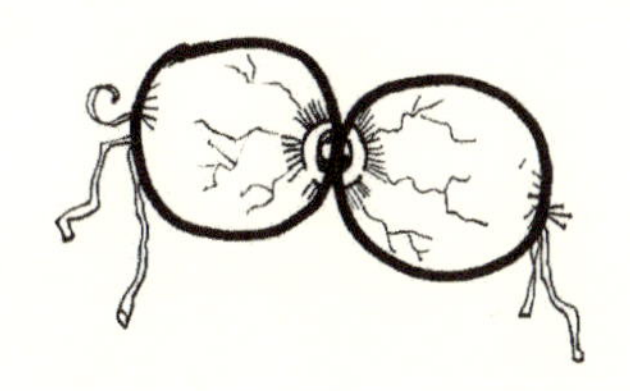

**_Tao Te Ching:_ 66. Lead by Following**

How does the river carve out the valley?
By flowing beneath it.
Thereby the river is master of the valley.
In order to master people
One must speak as their servant;
So when the sage is elevated to power
People do not feel oppressed.
In order to lead people
One must follow them;
So when the sage restrains people
They do not feel hindered.
Thus the popularity of the sage does not fail,
He does not seem superior, so no one will usurp him.

# 67. Three Wholes

It may seem that the Dude is a bum;
He takes it easy, so of course he achieves nothing;
If he achieved something he would long since have rolled another game.

Yet I have three treasures which I follow, and commend to you:
The first is abiding,
By which one does not worry.
The second is restraint,
By which one gets out of things cheap.
The third is not contending,
By which one provides comfort to strangers.

Those who are interested, but cannot abide,
Who mind, but without restraint,
Or who are fucking amateurs, yet threaten castration,
Enter a world of pain.

Only abiding conquers all, and is defeated by none.
It is Nature's heaviest bowling ball,
Its biggest scissors.
And its most simple plan.
A Swiss fucking watch.

***Tao Te Ching:* 67. Three Treasures**
It may seem that my teaching means nothing;
It describes the infinite, so of course it means nothing;
If it meant something it would long since have been refuted.
Yet I have three treasures which I follow and commend to you:
The first is love,
By which one finds courage.
The second is restraint,

By which one finds strength.
The third is not contending,
By which one finds influence.
Those who are fearless, but without love,
Strong, but without restraint,
Or influential, yet contentious,
Are doomed.
Only love conquers all and is defeated by none.
It is Nature's finest tool and sharpest weapon.

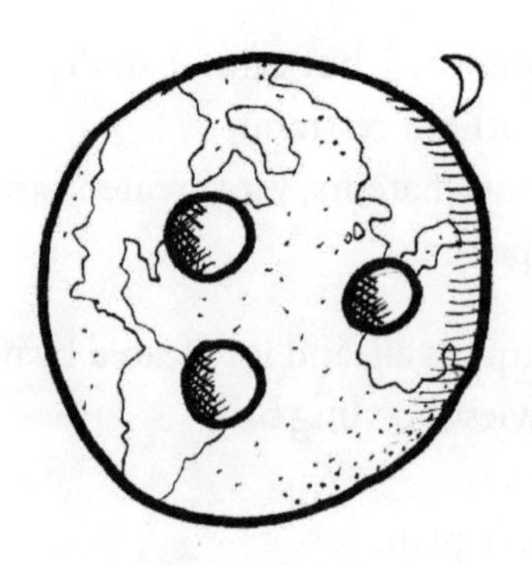

# 68. Take it Easy, Man

A good bowler does not contravene bylaws;
A good lord imagines where it goes from here;
A good buddy rests easy;
A good burger is found on a simple menu;
Not contending is the best way to have it your way, Dude.
And a good day to you, sir.

***Tao Te Ching:* 68. Using Men**

A good soldier does not use violence;
A good fighter does not use anger;
A good conqueror does not use attack;
A good ruler does not use authority;
Not contending is the best way to use men.

# 69. Combat

There is a saying among soldiers:
Fighting in the desert is much different than canopy jungle.

In this way one may deploy the ringer without having to take that hill,
Draw a line in the sand without stepping over the line,
Overcome amateurs without becoming bereaved,
And keep what's yours without getting a man down.

Conversely, there is no bummer like getting your dick cut off;
For bush-league psych-out stuff can get you fucked in the ass.
When two worthy fucking adversaries meet next Wednesday, baby,
The bowling team that is ready to be fucked
Will crack.

***Tao Te Ching:* 69. Ambush**
There is a saying among soldiers:
It is easier to lose a yard than take an inch.
In this way one may deploy troops without marshalling them,
Reveal weapons without exposing them,
Assault the foe without charging them,
Apply force without aggression.
Conversely there is no disaster like underestimating your enemy;
For false confidence will lose you your most valued assets.
When two equally matched forces meet
The general who conserves life will win.

# 70. The Parlance of our Times

The Dude's words are easy to understand
And the Dude's actions are easy to perform
But one must continually ask of him:
"What in God's holy name are you blathering about?"

The Dude's words have true sense;
The Dude's actions fit right in there;
You should try, like, listening, occasionally.
You might learn something.

We are each unique;
No man knows what the fuck the other is talking about.
Though the Dude wears an old bathrobe
His heart is green, with rust coloration.

***Tao Te Ching:* 70. Individuality**
My words are easy to understand
And my actions are easy to perform
Yet no man can understand or perform them.
My words have logic; my actions have meaning;
Yet these cannot be known and I cannot be known.
We are each unique; no man understands another.
Though the sage wears coarse clothes, his heart is jade.

# 71. Health problems

Who knows what he knows, can close the case on that one;
Who ignores what he ignores, is a goddamn moron;
Who grows sick of sickness, abides;
The Stranger is never sick,
Always sick of sickness.

***Tao Te Ching:* 71. Sickness**
Who knows what he knows is healthy;
Who ignores what he ignores is sick;
Who grows sick of sickness recovers;
The sage is never sick, always sick of sickness.

# 72. Doing Business

When strangers do not fear, they are ready to be fucked, man.
Praise their style,
And they will not dislike yours too, man.
Know your average,
But do not tell it to them;
Love your rug,
But do not let them know it tied the room together;
Let go of what is yours,
And take any rug in their house.

***Tao Te Ching:* 72. Diplomacy**
When people do not fear, they are easily conquered.
Praise their goods and children
And they will not dislike yours.
Know your advantage,
But do not tell it to them;
Love your home,
But do not let them know;
Reject what is yours
And accept what is theirs.

# 73. Your Roll

Who is brave and bold on Saturday may die;
Who is brave and subtle next Wednesday may live.
Which course best serves one's purpose?
Conflict favors some and destroys others.
Why? Well dude, we just don't know.

Dudeness does not contend, yet all things are conquered by it;
It does not ask, yet it is your answer for everything;
It does not call, it just walks through the unlocked door;
It does not plan, because its beauty is its simplicity.

Dudeness' hands are vast, its fingers spread so wide
That the world never slips through its grasp.

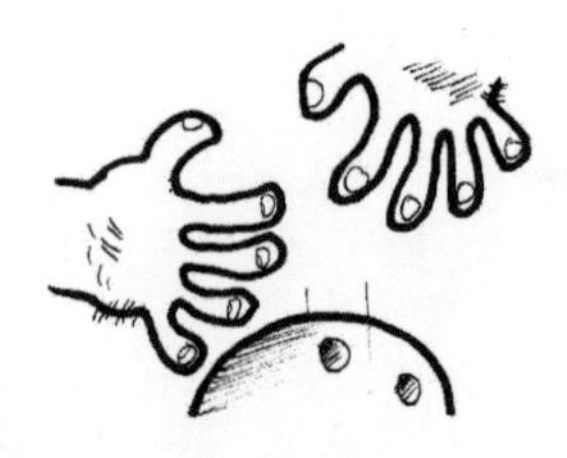

***Tao Te Ching:* 73. Fate**
Who is brave and bold may die;
Who is brave and subtle may live.
Which course best serves one's purpose?
Fate favours some and destroys others.
The sage does not know why.
Fate does not contend, yet all things are conquered by it;
It does not ask, yet all things answer to it;
It does not call, yet all things come to it;
It does not plan, yet all things are determined by it.
Fate's hands are vast, its fingers spread wide,
Yet none slip through its grasp.

# 74. Fascists

People need their johnsons, so do not threaten them with castration.
After you have met all the challenges, overcome all the obstacles,
And bested all the competitors in the world,
There would be no one left but you and the Nihilists;
And since they are fucking amateurs,
You would have to cut off your own johnson.

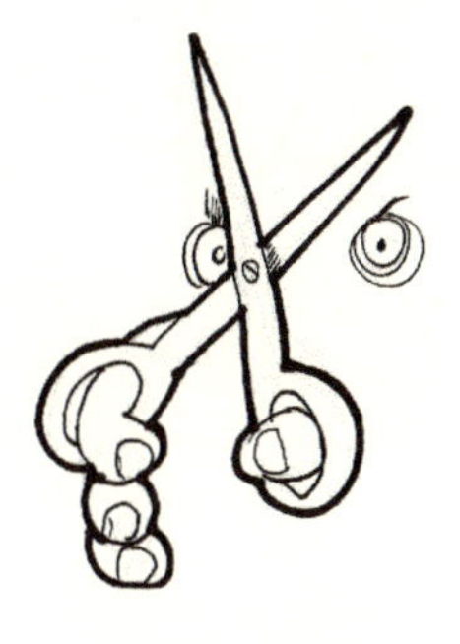

***Tao Te Ching:* 74. Tyranny**
People do not fear death, so do not threaten them with death.
If people feared death, and you executed all who did not love you
There would be no one left but you and the executioner.
You would then have to kill him.
You would then have to cut off your own hands.

# 75. Not Greedy

If rulers take too much fucking money,
People rapidly become goldbrickers;
If rulers soil too many rugs,
People easily feel they should be compensated;
If rulers take all the baksheesh,
People simply say "Fuck it, let's go bowling."

By not interfering, rich fucks can remain in seclusion.

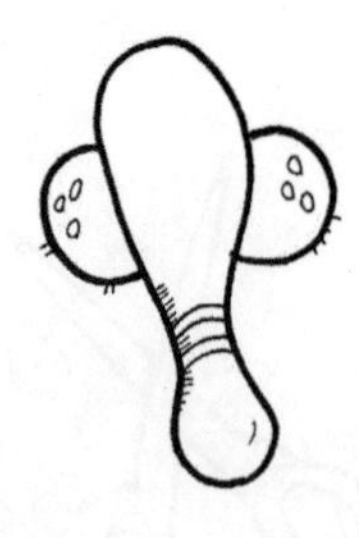

***Tao Te Ching:* 75. Extremis**
If rulers take too much grain
People rapidly starve;
If rulers take too much freedom
People easily rebel;
If rulers take too much happiness.
People gladly die.
By not interfering the sage improves the people's lives.

# 76. Limberness

A Dudeist's heart is soft and limber,
A Nihilist's heart is hard and rigid.
Plants and animals, while alive, are limber
And green, with some rust coloration;
In death, they are but smoke and ashes,
Stiff as a severed toe.
Thus softness and limberness are attributes of Dudeism,
And hardness and stiffness attributes of dipshits.

Just as a car parked in a handicapped spot will be towed,
So an adversary will meet defeat;
So many bright flowering young men died face down in
the muck;
In your wisdom you nixed 'em, Nixon,
While those who occupied various administration buildings
Still ably perform Dude-Jitsu upon their rugs.

***Tao Te Ching:* 76. Flexibility**

A newborn is soft and tender,
A crone, hard and stiff.
Plants and animals, in life, are supple and juicy;
In death, brittle and dry.
So softness and tenderness are attributes of life,
And hardness and stiffness, attributes of death.
Just as a sapless tree will split and decay
So an inflexible force will meet defeat;
The hard and mighty lie beneath the ground
While the tender and weak dance on the breeze above.

# 77. A Little of This, A Little of That

Is the movement of Nature not unlike bowling?
Everything rolls in cycles;
Toes that slip over the line do not enter the next round-robin;
A graceful approach, anticipation, strikes or gutters.
Given the nature of all this, are we going to split hairs?
Mark it eight, dude.

The Dude's way decreases those who have more than
they need,
And increases those who need more than they have.

It is not so with Jeffery Lebowski, the other Jeffery Lebowski.
He takes from those who are looking for a handout,
And gives to those whose allowance is already ample.

The Dude abides regardless of personal reward or recognition;
To benefit the World is to benefit the Dude, man;
See who benefits?
This affects all of us;
It's your roll.

***Tao Te Ching:* 77. Balance**
Is the movement of Nature not unlike drawing a bow?
What is higher descends and what is lower ascends;
What is longer shortens and what is shorter lengthens;
Nature's way decreases those who have more than they need
And increases those who need more than they have.
It is not so with Man.
Man decreases those who need more than they have
And increases those who have more than they need.
The sage works regardless of personal reward or recognition;
To benefit the World is to benefit the Self.

# 78. Have it Your Way, Dude

Nothing in the World takes it easier than water;
It is also good at cleaning pee-stains from a rug.

Just as the easy overcomes the uptight,
The bums may overcome the achievers;
Yet they do not.

The Stranger says:
"I like your style dude;
Just one thing, Dude—
D'ya have to use s'many cuss words?"

The fuck is he talking about?

***Tao Te Ching:* 78. Accept Responsibility**
Nothing in the World is as yielding as water;
Nor can anything better overcome the hardened.
Just as the yielding overcomes the hardened,
The weak may overcome the strong;
Yet they do not.
The sage says:
"Who accepts responsibility for his people rules the country;
Who accepts responsibility for the World rules the World",
But his words are not understood.

# 79. Wrapping 'er Up

Though the story is wrapped up, some what-have-yous remain—
How are you gonna keep 'em down on the farm?
What happened to the Dude's rug?
Did Maude compensate the Dude with bones or clams?
Well, Dude, we just don't know.

It don't matter to the Dudeist.
The Dude just wanted his rug back
And this guy peed on it;
For the Dude seeks harmony
Where justice seeks compensation.

The Stranger said: "He's the man for his time and place;
I won't say a hee-ro, cause what's a hee-ro?"
That done innerduced him enough.

***Tao Te Ching:* 79. Reconciliation**
When conflict is reconciled, some hatred remains;
How can this be put right?
The sage accepts less than is due
And does not blame or punish;
For love seeks agreement
Where justice seeks payment.
The saints said: "Nature is impartial;
Therefore it serves those who serve all."

# 80. Dudetopia

Imagine that there is a small bowling alley with few people;
Who have a hundred times bowled a perfect game;
Who love bowling and do not wander far;
Who own many balls but use only one;
Who have the necessary means but do not wave it around while threatening a world of pain;
Who love each other but face the fact that they're goddamn morons;
Who mix drinks well, dress comfortably, dwell in private residences,
And tie their rooms together without trying to scam anyone.

People in such a place would be very Dude.

***Tao Te Ching:* 80. Utopia**
Imagine that there is a small country with few people;
Who have a hundred times more than they need;
Who love life and do not wander far;
Who own ships but do no foreign trade;
Who own weapons but do not threaten war;
Who are literate but keep no histories;
Who cook well, dress beautifully, dwell safely
And delight in their own culture,
But live within cock crow of their neighbours.
People in such a place would never leave.

# 81. Friend

To tell you the truth, Brandt, I don't remember much;
Therefore there can be no literal connection;
This could be a uh, a lot more uh, uh, uh, uh, complex,
I mean it's not just, it might not be, just such a simple, uh—
you know?

A wiser feller than myself
Cannot be privy to all the new shit;
As for Nihilists, they're a bunch of fucking amateurs;
They need a manual to jerk off.

I've never been more certain of anything in my life:
The Dude does not look to get bumped into a higher bracket;
The more he takes it easy, the more he is satisfied;
And the more he abides the more he achieves.

The *Dude Way* is to treat everyone as a compeer,
Despite their wanderings.
For this whole fucking thing—it's only, just, like, our
opinion, man,
And we cannot drag this negative energy into the tournament.

In this way:
The Dude abides,
Down through the ages,
Across the sands of time,
With his johnson intact,
And a trophy life,
In the parlance of our times.

Fuckin' A Man.

***Tao Te Ching:* 81. The Sage**
Truth is not rhetorical;
Therefore rhetoric is not true;
Lovers do not contend;
Therefore competitors do not love;
The enlightened need no knowledge;
Therefore the learned are not enlightened.
The sage does not aim to increase himself;
But the more he does for others the more he is satisfied;
And the more he gives the more he gets.
The best way is to benefit all and harm none;
So the sage acheives his purpose without contention.